T0011375

States of Matter

by Daniel R. Faust

Consultant: Sara Vogt
Science Educator at Anoka Hennepin School District

BEARPORT
PUBLISHING

Minneapolis, Minnesota

Credits

Cover and title page, © sandsun/iStock, © Nlshop/Shutterstock and © Stone36/Shutterstock; 4, © Cherdchai charasri/Shutterstock and © Boris Medvedev/Shutterstock; 5, © donatas1205/Shutterstock and © Andrey_Kuzmin/Shutterstock; 8, © Abramova Kseniya/Shutterstock; 11, © palonezn/Shutterstock; 13, © TommyB_Photo/Shutterstock; 14, © VladaKela/Shutterstock; 15, © Kirill Tonkikh/Shutterstock; 17, © Halil ibrahim mescioglu/Shutterstock; 19, © Robert Kyllo/Shutterstock; 21, © Oleg_Yakovlev/Shutterstock; 23T, © Gadzick/Shutterstock; 23B, © Teri Virbickis/Shutterstock; 25TL, © Captured by Nicole/Shutterstock; 25TR, © Teerapong Teerapong/Shutterstock; 25BL, © Nickeline/Shutterstock; 25BR, © Mario Toth/Shutterstock; and 27, © YouraPechkin/Shutterstock.

Bearport Publishing Company Product Development Team

President: Jen Jenson; Director of Product Development: Spencer Brinker; Senior Editor: Allison Juda; Editor: Charly Haley; Associate Editor: Naomi Reich; Senior Designer: Colin O'Dea; Associate Designer: Elena Klinkner; Associate Designer: Kayla Eggert; Product Development Assistant: Anita Stasson

Library of Congress Cataloging-in-Publication Data is available at www.loc.gov or upon request from the publisher.

ISBN: 979-8-88509-426-9 (hardcover)
ISBN: 979-8-88509-548-8 (paperback)
ISBN: 979-8-88509-663-8 (ebook)

For more information, write to Bearport Publishing, 5357 Penn Avenue South, Minneapolis, MN 55419.

Contents

It All Matters

The air you breathe, your favorite drink, and your school books are all made of **matter**. So, why can't you hold on to air? Why doesn't your drink stay in a glass that's tipped over? Sometimes, it's the **state** of matter that matters!

All matter can be measured. Mass tells the amount of stuff in something. Volume is the amount of space it takes up. Two things with the same volume can have very different masses.

Making Matter

Everything around us is matter, and all matter is made of **atoms**. Atoms can be broken down even more. A nucleus sits at the center of each atom. It is made of protons and neutrons. Little electrons travel around the nucleus.

Not all atoms are the same. Different kinds of atoms have different numbers of protons, neutrons, and electrons. This means things made of different atoms look and act differently.

A Model of an Atom

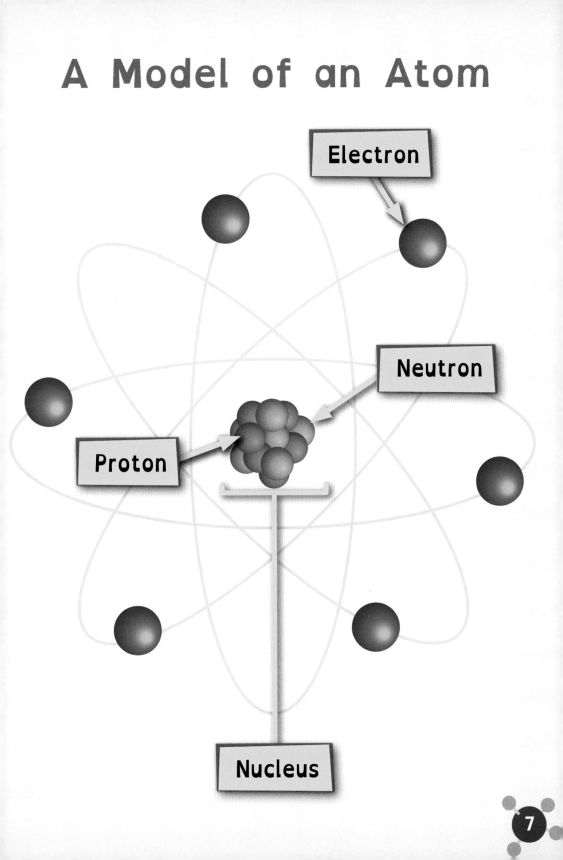

Electron

Neutron

Proton

Nucleus

Some matter is made of a single atom. Other times, atoms come together. **Molecules** form when two or more atoms share electrons. They bond, or stick together, through these electrons. The more atoms that come together, the bigger the molecule they make.

Whether they are in a big lake or tiny raindrop, all the molecules of water are the same. There are just more of them in a lake.

A Model of a Water Molecule

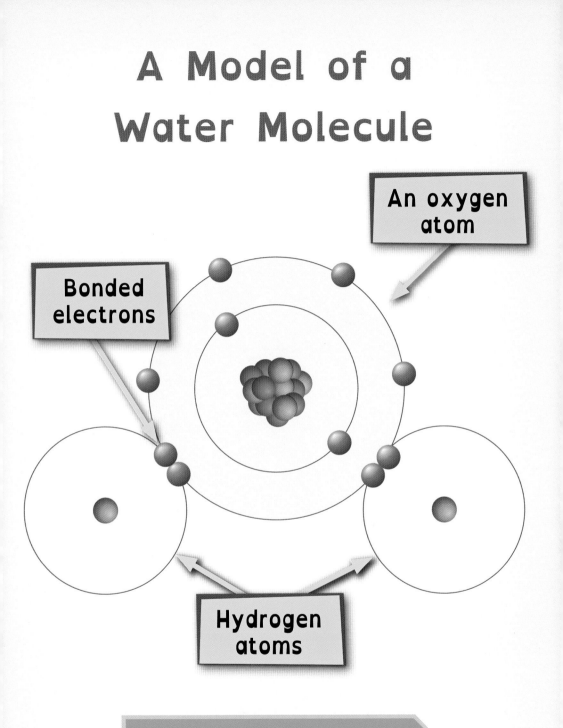

An oxygen atom

Bonded electrons

Hydrogen atoms

Hydrogen and oxygen atoms form water molecules.

In a State

Matter on Earth exists in three main forms, or states. They are solid, liquid, and gas. In each state, the molecules within matter act differently.

Their behavior is based on two properties. The first is attraction. All molecules are drawn to one another.

The attraction between molecules is weaker when there is more space between them. This amount of space is different in each state of matter.

The second property is **motion**. Molecules are always moving. At lower temperatures, molecules move more slowly. When they are hot, molecules move very quickly.

If molecules move fast enough, they can break any attraction between them. Then, the molecules move apart.

For most matter, when molecules are cold they move slowly. In fact, sometimes they can only shake in place. They are still moving, but you cannot see it with your eyes.

Molecules in boiling water move quickly.

Solid and Sturdy

Sometimes, molecules are attracted close together. They move very slowly. These molecules make up an object in the solid state. Because they are packed in so tightly, solid objects are **rigid**. They do not change size or shape easily.

The molecules in many solids are bonded in repeating patterns. This locks the molecules in place. They are a lot like bricks in a sturdy wall. The molecules cannot be easily separated.

Go with the Flow

Molecules in a liquid move faster than those in a solid. However, they do not move fast enough to break the attraction between them. Instead, the molecules slide past one another. This allows liquids to change their shape easily. Often, they take on the shape of their container.

Different liquids move at different speeds. Some liquids, such as water, flow very easily. They change shape quickly. Others are thick and slow-moving.

Honey is liquid, but it does not flow easily.

It's a Gas

The molecules in a gas move very quickly. They get very far apart from one another. The shape and volume of a gas can change easily. Like a liquid, a gas will take the shape of its container. It will also expand to fill that space.

There is a lot of empty space between molecules in a gas. Sometimes, we push the molecules closer together. This makes it easier to package gas so we can take it where we want it.

Helium in a tank is pushed together. It expands outside the tank to fill a balloon.

Out of This World

There is a fourth state of matter called **plasma**, but you'd have to travel far to find it. We don't usually find things in this state on Earth. Like gas, plasma changes shape and volume easily. However, plasma exists at only extremely high temperatures.

Plasma is most commonly found in stars. One of the few times we can see it on Earth is during a thunderstorm. Lightning is a form of plasma.

A lightning bolt can be five times hotter than the surface of the sun.

Changing States

Matter can change from one state to another. To do this, the molecules need to move faster or slower than they already are. Taking in energy makes molecules move more quickly. Matter can also lose energy, which makes the molecules move more slowly.

Heat is the most common form of energy that makes matter change state. Leave a candy bar in the sun or stick an ice cream treat in the freezer. What happens?

Melting happens when a solid takes in energy. It becomes a liquid. When a liquid gets enough energy to become a gas, it is called evaporation (i-*vap*-uh-RAY-shuhn). A gas can lose energy and turn into a liquid in condensation (*kahn*-den-SAY-shuhn). A loss of energy in a liquid turns it solid. That's freezing.

Matter usually needs to pass through one state on its way to another. However, sometimes a solid can become a gas without being a liquid first. This is called sublimation (*suh*-bleh-MAH-shuhn).

The Matter at Hand

Matter may look different when it takes in or lets out energy. Molecules behave differently in different states. They spread apart and move faster. Yet the molecules that make up the matter are the same from state to state. The more things change, the more they stay the same.

No matter if it is steam or ice, water is always made up of the same kinds of molecules. They are two hydrogen atoms bonded to one oxygen atom.

Matter in Many States

Solid

- Molecules in solids are packed tightly together.
- They hold their shape, and they do not move very much.

Liquid

- Liquids are packed a little more loosely.
- They can move or flow around to become the shape of their container.
- The parts of a liquid move around more than in solids.

Gas

- Gases move around the most.
- Their molecules are spread out.
- A gas can fill up an entire space.

★ SilverTips for REVIEW

Review what you've learned. Use the text to help you.

Define key terms

gas   molecule

liquid   solid

matter

Check for understanding

What are the two main properties of all molecules?

What are the three main states of matter found on Earth?

How does matter change from one state to another, and what are the names for these processes?

Think deeper

Think of a solid, a liquid, and a gas you see every day. How might each of these things be different in another state?

★ SilverTips on TEST-TAKING

- **Make a study plan.** Ask your teacher what the test is going to cover. Then, set aside time to study a little bit every day.

- **Read all the questions carefully.** Be sure you know what is being asked.

- **Skip any questions** you don't know how to answer right away. Mark them and come back later if you have time.

Glossary

atoms the tiny building blocks that make up every substance in the universe

attraction a force that pulls something toward something else

matter the material that makes up all objects

molecules small things made from groups of atoms

motion movement

plasma a state of matter that exists at very high temperatures and is not often found on Earth

properties the ways things look or act

rigid firm or stiff

state a way or form of being

Read More

Biskup, Agnieszka. *The Solid Truth about States of Matter with Max Axiom, Super Scientist: 4D An Augmented Reading Science Experience (Graphic Science 4D).* North Mankato, MN: Capstone Press, 2019.

Gardner, Jane Parks. *Matter (Intro to Physics: Need to Know).* Minneapolis: Bearport Publishing Company, 2023.

Griffin, Mary. *States of Matter (A Look at Chemistry).* New York: Gareth Stevens, 2019.

Learn More Online

1. Go to **www.factsurfer.com** or scan the QR code below.

2. Enter "**States of Matter**" into the search box.

3. Click on the cover of this book to see a list of websites.

Index

About the Author

Daniel R. Faust is a freelance writer of fiction and nonfiction. He lives in Brooklyn, NY.